THE REVERSE COLORING BOOK™

Through the Seasons

Kendra Norton

Workman Publishing
New York

REVERSE COLORING IDEAS

Not sure where to start? Try some of these ideas and see where they take you!

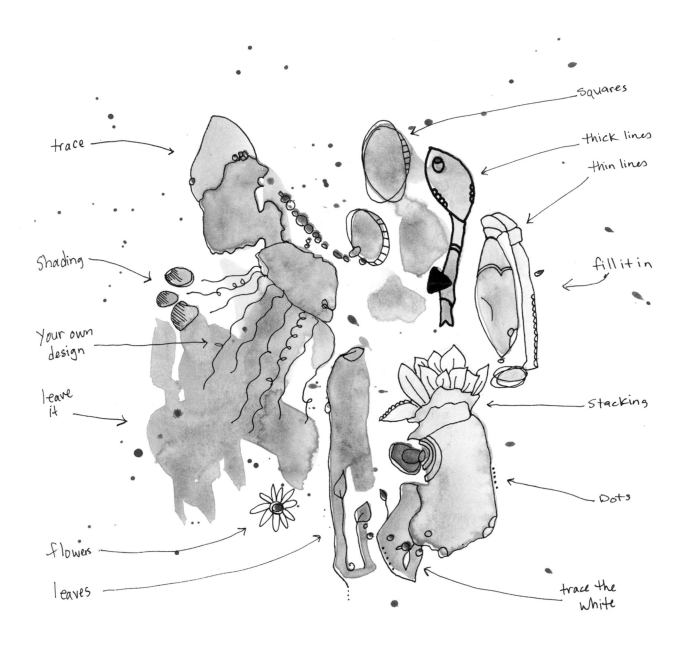

trace

squares

thick lines

thin lines

Shading

Your own design

fill it in

leave it

Stacking

flowers

Dots

leaves

trace the white

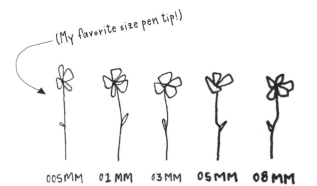

(My favorite size pen tip!)

005MM   01MM   03MM   05MM   08MM

THERE ARE NO RULES! You can use any pen you like. I use felt tip, non-bleeding, permanent ink pens. They look similar to the one depicted on the cover. They come in a variety of sizes and colors. Experiment with a few to see what you love best!

*Creativity can be described as
a letting go of certainties.
—Gail Sheehy*

Welcome to the second Reverse Coloring Book—*Through the Seasons*!

You'll notice that the colors and shapes resemble the seasons, moving from spring to summer; fall to winter. Mix up the seasons with your own shapes and ideas—or try combining them. Snowflakes in summer and daisies in winter! There's no limit to what you can come up with, you creative genius! Let these pages unlock and inspire your imagination and your mindfulness. There are no rules here. Break the nonexistent rules! Make new rules and break those too. Have fun and just keep going.

I love seeing pages shared on Instagram and TikTok at #thereversecoloringbook. Whenever I see a painting made unique with another artist's drawings or doodles, I get a feeling of creative resolution, like the last note of a song after a pause in the music. It truly warms my heart to collaborate with so many creatives around the world.

So grab a pen and find a corner of the world to make some lines!

With love, always,

Kendra Norton

P.S. Stay connected with me on Instagram @kendranortonart to see what I am up to.

SPRING

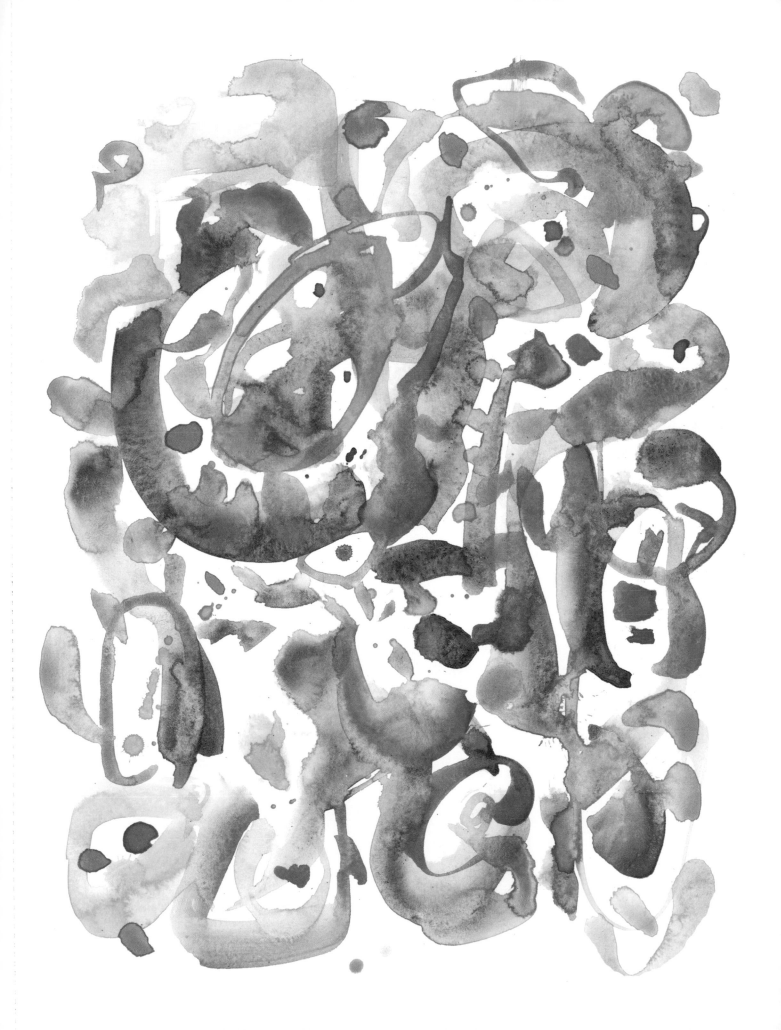

SUMMER

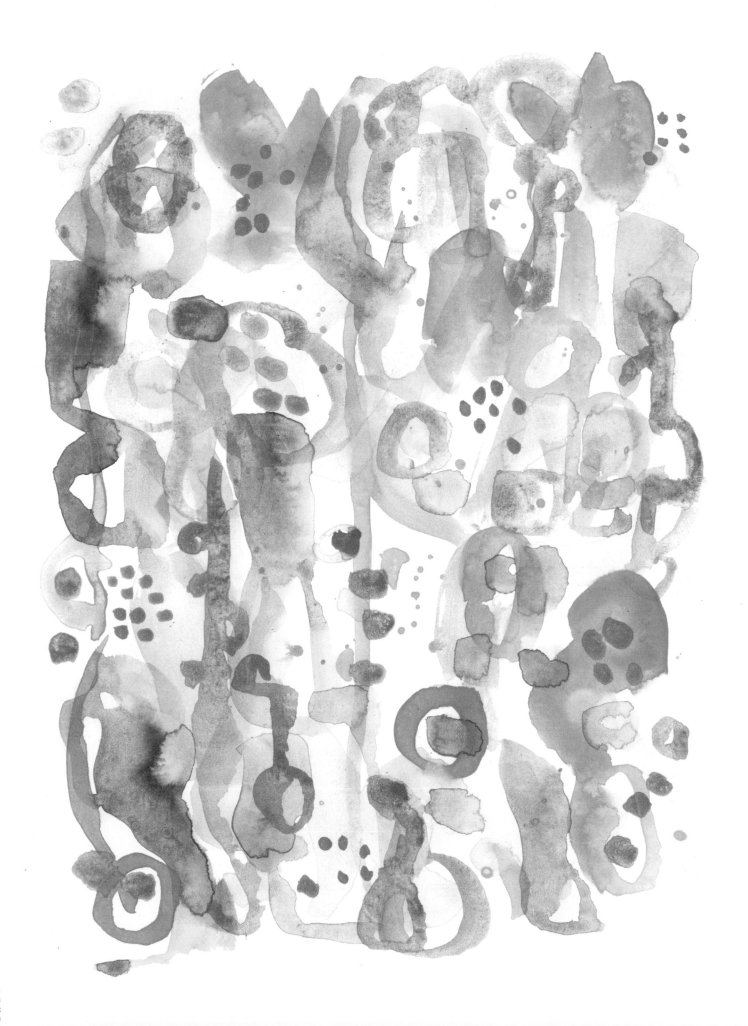

FALL

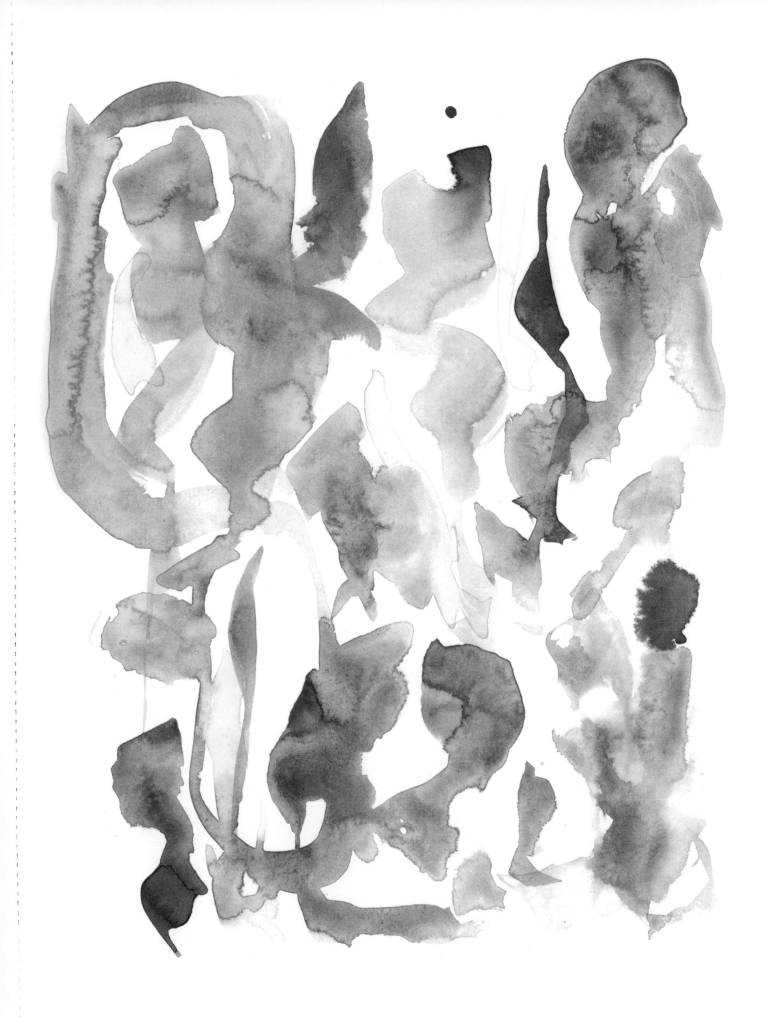

WINTER

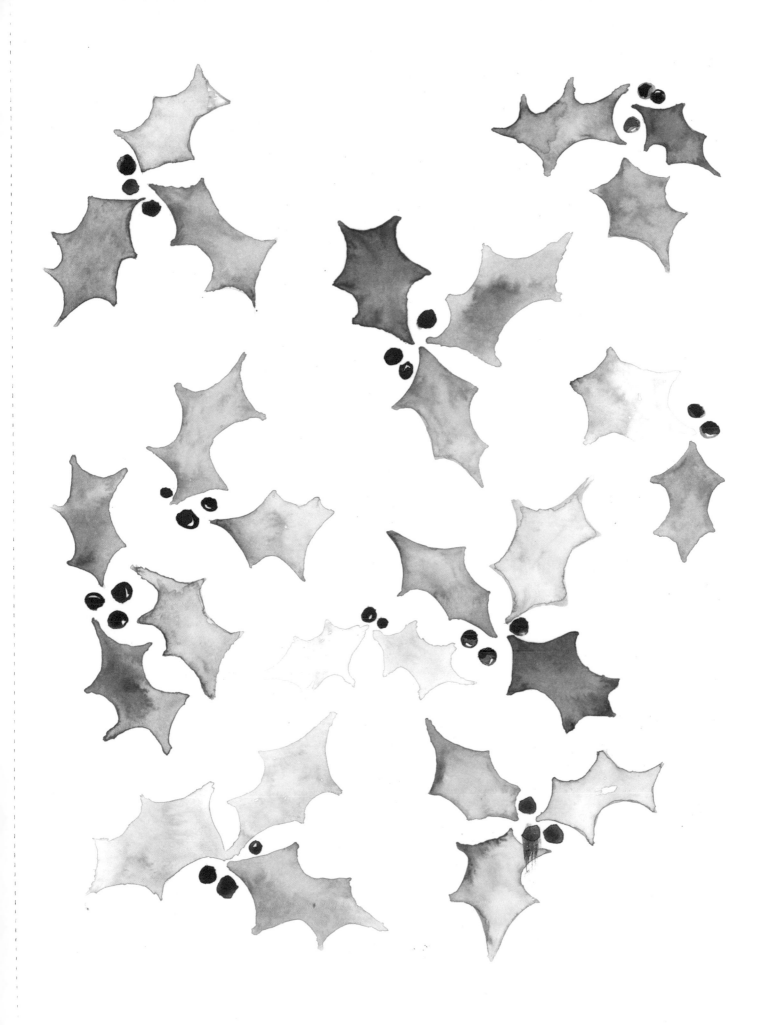

ISBN 978-1-5235-1528-8

Design by Becky Terhune

Workman books are available at special discounts when purchased in bulk for premiums and sales
promotions as well as for fundraising or educational use. Special editions or book excerpts can also be
created to specification. For details, contact the Special Sales Director at specialmarkets@workman.com.

Workman Publishing Co., Inc.
225 Varick Street
New York, NY 10014-4381

workman.com

THE REVERSE COLORING BOOK is a trademark of Kendra Norton.
WORKMAN is a registered trademark of Workman Publishing Co., Inc.

Printed in China on paper from responsible sources
First printing April 2022

10 9 8 7 6 5 4 3 2